The Art of
Food Sculpture
Designs & Techniques

Yuci Tan

4880 Lower Valley Road, Atglen, PA 19310 USA

Published by Schiffer Publishing Ltd.
4880 Lower Valley Road
Atglen, PA 19310
Phone: (610) 593-1777; Fax: (610) 593-2002
E-mail: Schifferbk@aol.com
Please visit our web site catalog at **www.schifferbooks.com**
We are always looking for people to write books on new and related
subjects. If you have an idea for a book, please contact us at the above
address.

This book may be purchased from the publisher.
Include $3.95 for shipping.
Please try your bookstore first.
You may write for a free catalog.

In Europe, Schiffer books are distributed by
Bushwood Books
6 Marksbury Avenue
Kew Gardens
Surrey TW9 4JF England
Phone: 44 (0) 20 8392 8585
Fax: 44 (0) 20 8392 9876
E-mail: Bushwd@aol.com
Free postage in the UK. Europe: air mail at cost.

Library of Congress Cataloging-in-Publication Data

Tan, Yuci, 1955-
    The art of food sculpture : designs & techniques/Yuci Tan.
        p. cm.
ISBN 0-7643-1454-8
1. Garnishes(Cookery).2. Cookery(Cold dishes) 3. Food
presentation. 4. Table setting and decoration. I. Title.
TX740.5.T36 2001
641.5-dc21
                                                    2001003938

Designed by John P. Cheek
Cover design by Bruce M. Waters
Type set in Van Dijk(bolded)/Dutch801 Rm BT

ISBN: 0-7643-1454-8
Printed in China

Dedication

I dedicate this book to all those I love and who love me.

Foreword

This book is intended to be a step-by-step practical manual for food decoration and garnishing. It illustrates the basic techniques of exquisite food sculpture and garnishing in both the Chinese and American styles, using common vegetables and fruits available in supermarkets and grocery stores.

The first chapter illustrates the tools used in food sculpture, while the second chapter provides step-by-step instruction in the basic food sculpture skills. Each step is illustrated for the beginner, using sample projects for skill development. The following chapters provide drawings and explanatory notes showing the steps of execution. These chapters are organized according to the materials used. The final chapters of the book address the needs of fancy restaurants and hotels specializing in parties and banquets. Special sections illustrate ideas for garnishing hors d'oeuvres trays, fruit trays, cold meat trays, tea sandwich trays, vegetable trays, and seafood trays. For large pieces of food sculpture, I provide designs for different functions or banquets, such as weddings, birthdays, anniversaries, Christmas, New Years, Independence Day, Thanksgiving, Halloween, and buffet receptions based on my field experiences working in large American hotels and country clubs. Finally, stencils are provided to aid you in your melon design.

This book is an excellent resource for self-study, as well as a practical textbook for culinary art programs. Readers will surely appreciate the unique user-friendly features of this book, rarely found in books of similar nature.

I am deeply grateful to Mr. James A. Moll and Mr. Chester J. Qian. Especially Mr. Moll who, as a food-purchasing manager, not only edited my book but also provided me with a lot of product knowledge. Without their cooperation and help, the preparation of the current book for publication would not have been possible. I also give great thanks to my daughter Xiaoyu Yang who has been so supportive and has given me many positive suggestions.

Table of Contents

Chapter 1
Food Sculpture Tools

Most of these tools should be available locally from kitchen and art supply stores, or you can purchase them directly from the author. Contact her at yucitan@yahoo.com.

Sculpture Tools

These are the general tools you will need for all your carving projects. The six tools shown on the left are special food sculpture tools. The two left-most tools are called "edging tools" and are used for carving distinct edges of designs. The middle two tools are called "V-carving tools" and come in many different sizes. They are used for making v-shaped grooves. The fifth is called a "U-carving tool," which also comes in many different sizes and is used for making U-shaped grooves, making depressions and feathers. The sixth tool is called a "hole maker." It comes in many different sizes and is used for making holes and columns. The four knives shown at right are usually used for cutting large material, cheese and tallow carving, flower carvings, and very fine parts respectively.

Melon Carving Tools

These tools are actually wood carving tools. They are perfect for carving melons. Besides V-carving and U-carving tools, there are different sizes of chisels. They are used for removing melon skin and are very useful.

Dough Sculpture Tools

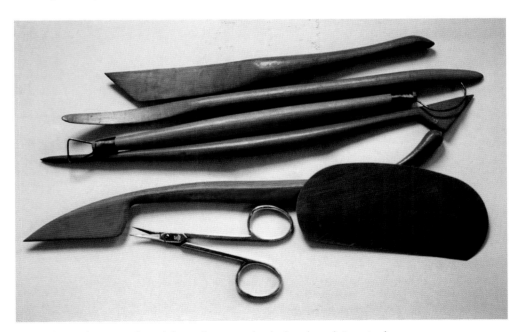

Clay sculpture tools and fine scissors are basic dough sculpture tools.

Chapter 2
Basic Food Sculpture Techniques

These techniques include three methods, they are: the rolling or folding and securing method, the three dimensional scuplture method, and the taking advantage of natural colors and shapes method. If you follow these step-by-step procedures (and practice, practice, practice) you will be able to carve almost anything you want.

Rolling or Folding and Securing Method

This method is the easiest one. Choose round and solid material for this kind of garnish. Carrots, turnips, potatoes, beets, cucumbers, acorn squashes, daikon radishes, parsnips, Canadian bacon, salami, ham, and turkey lunchmeat are all candidates for rolling and folding. First slice the material, then roll or fold the slices, finally use a toothpick to secure them.

Chrysanthemum

You can use any kind of lunchmeat or vegetable that can made into rectangular slices. Here I use ham.

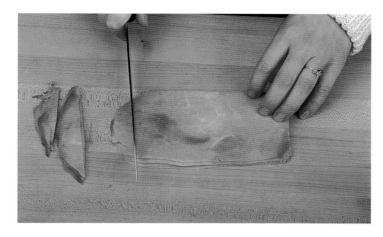

Slice the ham and cut five slices into rectangles.

Cut 1/4-inch strips 3/4 of the way through the short side of the rectangle.

Finish the whole slice. Cut one thin carrot slice the same way.

Place the carrot slice on top of two ham slices. Start rolling.

Add two more ham slices, and continue rolling.

Add the last ham slice, and roll it as well.

Secure the uncut end with toothpicks.

Turn the face up.

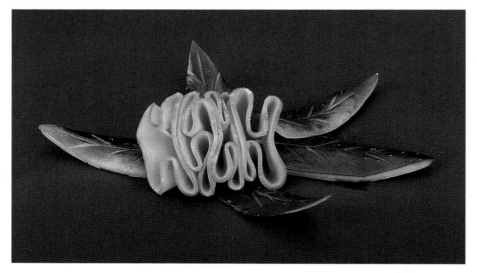

You can use any kind of cylinder-shaped lunchmeat or vegetables. Such as Canadian bacon, hard salami, bologna, beets, carrots, cucumbers, or turnips. Here I use Canadian bacon.

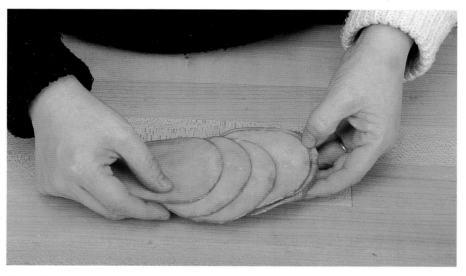

You will need three to five slices of ham, depending on the thickness, and cherry tomatoes.

Fold the slices as shown.

Secure with a toothpick.

Add cherry tomatoes to the tips of toothpicks; turn face up.

Three Dimensional Sculpture Method

This method is the hardest one. Use textured hard and solid materials for this garnish, such as thick slices of pumpkin meat, daikon radishes, sweet potatoes, turnips, large carrots, butternut squashes, and small melons. The basic steps are:

1. Choose the medium based on the design.
2. Carve an outline on the material.
3. Fine-sculpt the outline until finished.

The three-dimensional sculpture method includes the straight carving method, the rotated carving method, and the animal carving method.

Straight Carving Method

This method only needs straight cuts with a regular paring knife.

Poinsettia Candleholder

Cut the end of a cantaloupe so it will sit stable.

Carve the design of three leaves just through the skin with an edging tool.

Cut under the leaves to disengage them with a paring knife.

Leave them attached at the base.

Smooth the leaves with a knife.

Sculpt the interior of the leaves with a V-carving tool.

Remove about 1/3 off the top of the cantaloupe and remove the seeds.

Remove the remaining skin.

Carve five petals out
of the remaining meat
area.

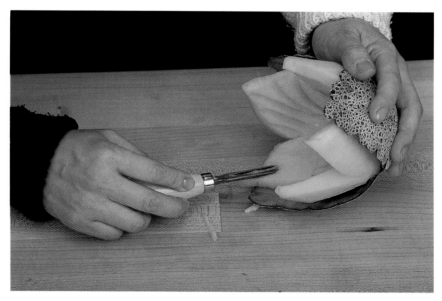

Sculpt the interior of the petals with a U-carving tool.

Carve a hole in the middle of the base to hold a long candle.

Rotated Carving Method

The rotated carving method is used for carving special flower petal shapes such as the petals of tulips and magnolias. It requires patience and practice. Use a very sharp, fine, and pointy paring knife. Hold the knife at almost a 90-degree angle to the surface and very carefully carve the petals by rotating the wrist.

Beautiful Tulip

A section of daikon radish, a perfect material for carving flowers and animals.

Cut a three-inch section of Daikon and carve into an egg-shape.

Holding the paring knife at a 60-degree angle to the side, carve the first petal.

In the same way, carve the first row of petals.

Remove the rough material to make it smooth again.

Hold the paring knife at a 90-degree angle and carve a petal by rotating the wrist.

Carve an interior petal.

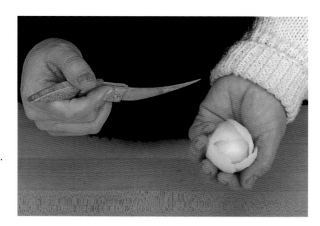

Remove the rough material under the petal.

Continue carving until the center is reached.

Animal Carving Method

The carving materials and steps for beasts, birds, and fish are similar to the three-dimensional sculpting technique, the only difference being the carving of bird feathers and fish scales. Bird feather carving is analogous to fish scale carving except feathers are longer than scales. I usually use different size U-carving tools and a sharp knife for this carving. Here I use a very simple carving example to explain how to carve them.

Fish Tray Garnish

Shape a fish head out of a jicama.

Carve a mouth with a paring knife.

Carve a gill with a V-carving tool.

Make a depression for the eye with a U-carving tool.

Carve scales on the gill. (Details below)

Sculpt the fin.

Shape a fish tail out of a jicama.

Carve a row of scales on the tail with a U-carving tool.

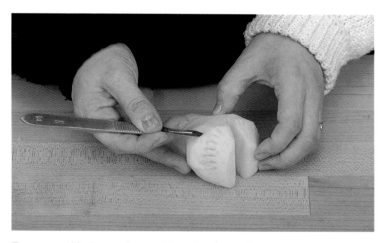

Remove a thin layer of material under the scales.

Continue carving alternating rows of scales to the fin.

Taking Advantage of Natural Colors and Shapes Method

This method is different from the three-dimensional sculpture method in that it uses the natural vegetable or fruit shape instead of carving the initial shape at the beginning. It is easy to learn and the results are lively and vivid. This book offers a few examples (person, flower, animal, bird, and fish) by way of introduction, so that you may create your own designs. Remember, when you design this kind of garnish, try to use the vegetable or the fruit's original color and shape as much as you can.

Frog

Cut a green zucchini in half at a slight angle.

Remove a wedge near the end for a mouth.

Cut three quarter-inch slices at the bottom, but not all the way through.

Cut the slices in half, but again, not all the way through.

Cut through the skin in the front to create the stomach design.

Remove the skin to represent the frog's belly and arms with a small chisel.

Smooth the carved area.

Separate the half slices for feet and hold in place with a toothpick.

Attach grapes with toothpicks to create eyes. If you want to add a tongue, cut a small chip of carrot and secure in mouth using a piece of toothpick.

Penguin

Cut a yellow squash in half.

Cut through the skin in the front to create the stomach design.

Use a small chisel to remove the skin and create the penguin's belly and face.

Smooth the carved area.

Shape the feet.

Carve the toes on the feet with a V-carving tool.

Carve a hole in the face with a U-carving tool and insert a black peppercorn for the eye.

Golfer

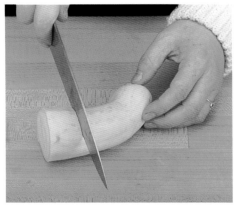

Choose a curved yellow squash
for this garnish. Cut it in half.

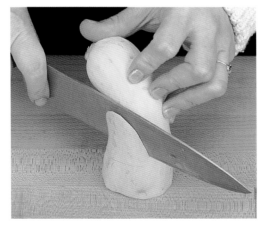

Cut off a piece on
each side for arms.

Carve one slice of carrot.

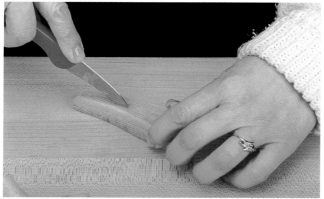
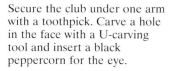

Carve a golf club out of the carrot slice.

Secure the club under one arm with a toothpick. Carve a hole in the face with a U-carving tool and insert a black peppercorn for the eye.

Bokchoy Rose

Cut away the leaves. You will need about 2 inches of the stem from a head of bokchoy.

Shape petals using the base of the leaves.

Continue shaping from the outside stems to the inside stems.

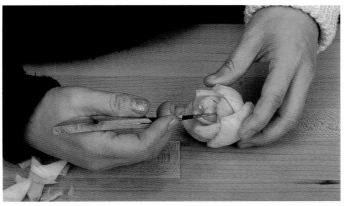

Remove the interior portions of each petal to make them thin. Slide a bamboo skewer inside a scallion to use as a stem. Attach fresh herbs to the base for leaves.

Angel Fish

Cut one third from the side of an apple.

Create the shape of the angel fish.

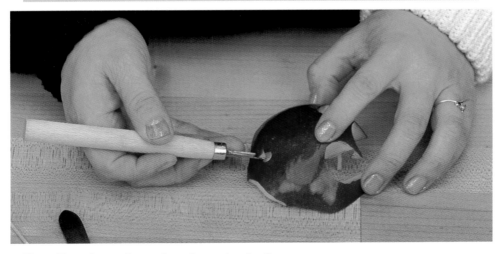

Use a U-carving tool to make a depression for the eye.

Use a V-carving tool to sculpt the fins and scales. Soak carved portions of apple with lemon juice to delay browning effect. Mount the fish on a zucchini base using toothpicks and add scallions or other fresh herbs for seaweed.

Tropical fish.

Cut one third of an apple and cut out a tropical fish shape.

Carve a mouth with a U-shaped carving tool.

Carve a depression large enough for a half grape where the eye should be.

Insert a half grape.

Sculpt the fins with a V-shaped carving tool.

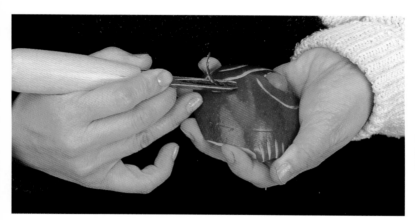

Carve scales with the V-shaped carving tool.

Mount the fish on a zucchini base using toothpicks and add scallions or other herbs for seaweed. Soak the carved portions of the apple with lemon juice to delay browning.

Melon Carving Techniques

Melon carving is totally different from other fruits and vegetables. Melons come in all sorts of textures, colors, shapes, and sizes, and require various carving skills. This allows for a great diversity of finished products.

Generally speaking there are two kinds of melon carvings: lanterns or candleholders, and containers. Both play very important roles at parties and buffets. The former is found at the beginning of a party or buffet. It likes the appetizer course. Its color and beauty can increase guests' appetites. The latter is found at the end of the party or buffet, and is perfect with desserts. It can be a perfect fruit salad container. There are also three different basic techniques including the relief, hollow, and lantern technique.

Relief Sculpture Technique

This technique requires carving a design on a melon surface. Use the contrasting colors of the melon skin and meat to accentuate the design.

This carving skill is easier than the hollow sculpture technique, but needs good drawing skills so that you can use a knife instead of a pen on the melon surface. V-carving tools, U-carving tools, and chisels are used for this technique.

Oak Tree Candleholder or Container

This carving can hold several candles and/or be used as a container for fruit salad.

Stabilize a cantaloupe by making a flat cut on the bottom. Carve the outline of a tree trunk and branches through the skin.

Use a chisel to remove the skin, leaving the skin intact where the trunk, branches, and leaves will be.

Smooth the carved areas.

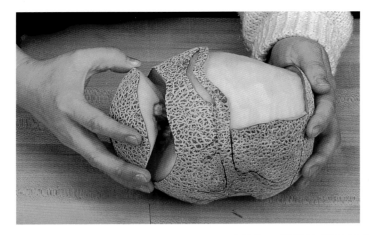

Cut an uneven line to simulate the top of the tree, and remove the very top. Scoop out the seeds.

Scrape away the very thin, outer-most part of the skin around the upper rim, where the leaves will be, allowing the dark green inner skin to show.

Carve the leaves in the dark green area.

Use a U-carving tool to make several holes, about an inch deep, to hold the candles.

Hollow Sculpture Technique

This technique takes the relief sculpture one step further. After carving the relief sculpture, some of the areas are completely removed.

Hosta Lantern

Cut off the top of a
honeydew and scrape out
the flesh, reducing the
thickness by about two-
thirds.

Cut the design into the melon
approximately a quarter-inch deep.

Remove the outer skin.

47

Cut out the design following the incisions you made earlier.

Shape the leaves with a V-carving tool.

Special Lantern Sculpture Technique

This is a special Chinese style technique. There are three parts to carve. The first is only cut through the skin, the second is only cut through the meat but not the skin, and the last is cut all the way through. This technique creates interlocking hooks in the skin allowing for wonderful three-dimensional designs. When lit from inside, the effects can be dazzling.

Honeydew Lantern

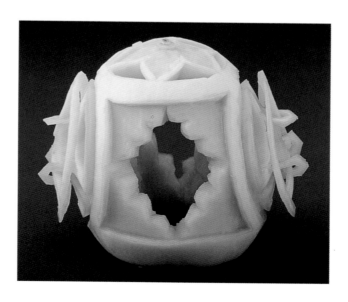

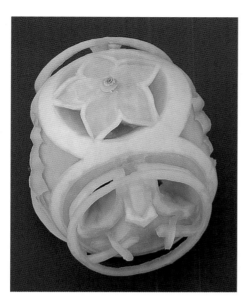

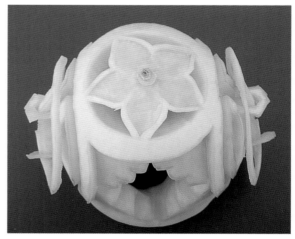

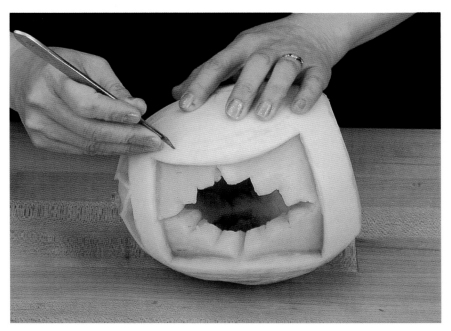

Stabilize a honeydew by making a flat cut on one end and remove the seeds. Cut a simple design on top and on two sides before carving the lantern. Cut the outline of the design through the skin only.

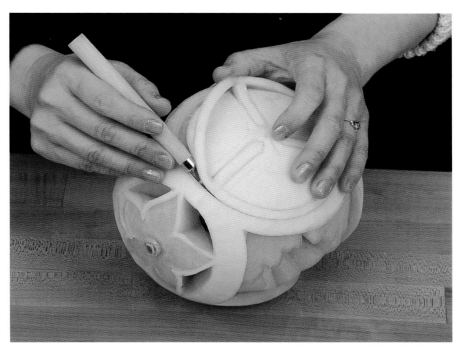

Pierce the skin only with a small chisel.

Loosen the whole ring and inner three flaps half way.

Cut the three middle flaps through the meat from the inside.

Cut through the other half flaps' skin with a knife and loosen them with the chisel.

Cut through the meat (meat only, keep the skin on) right across the three flaps with the chisel.

Push out from the inside to produce the three-dimensional lantern design.

Put the three-dimensional lantern design back when storing it to prevent drying out. Repeat the above steps to carve another three-dimensional lantern design on the other side.

Mixed Technique

In real life, most food sculpture requires multiple techniques. As you see, on the honeydew lantern, the three-dimensional lantern design uses the special melon lantern sculpture technique, and the top and side designs use both the relief and hollow sculpture techniques.

Orchids

Orchids are a sample of mixed techniques. The straight carving method and rotated carving method both are used in this work.

Carefully cut around the stem and seeds of a red bell pepper.

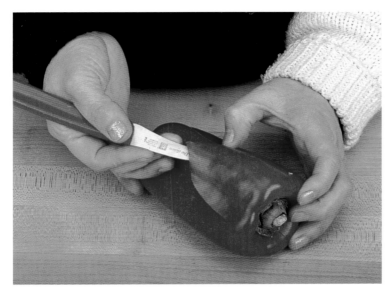

Carve three petals around the pepper cutting completely through the skin.

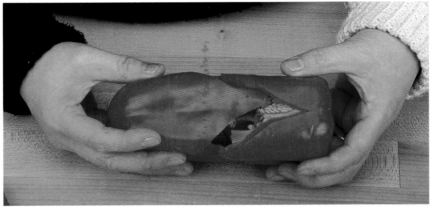

Remove the seeds and white interior.

Slice each petal into two layers.

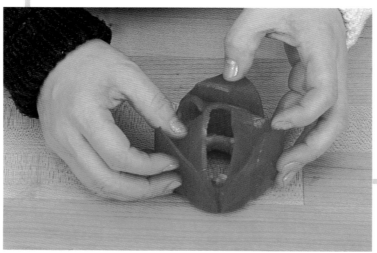

Start with an egg-shaped piece of Daikon radish and carve it the same as a tulip. Put inside the pepper petals and, using a long skewer plant the flower in a thick slice of jicama, and use a piece of squash for a base.

Chapter 3
Simple Vegetable Carving

These kinds of carvings are used for decorating various kinds of dinner plates, appetizer, and salad plates in everyday restaurant operations. They may also be used to garnish and decorate hors d'oeuvre plates, pâté platters and vegetable trays for parties of various sizes. Some of them may also be used as containers for dips and dressings.

Okra

Plum Blossom

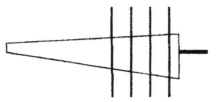

Crosscut okra into eighth-inch slices for flowers.

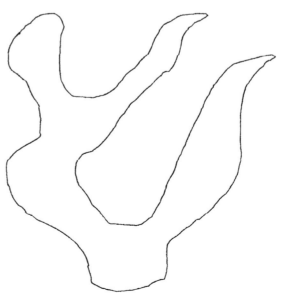

Carve a trunk and branches out of a piece of carrot.

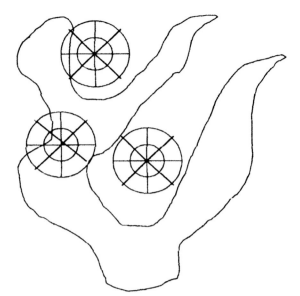

Assemble by anchoring the okra slices to the trunk with toothpicks.

Vegetable Stems

Clematis

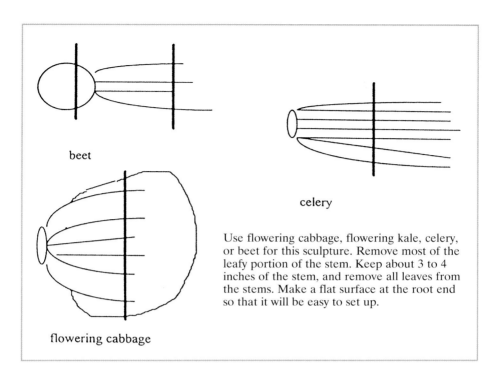

beet

celery

flowering cabbage

Use flowering cabbage, flowering kale, celery, or beet for this sculpture. Remove most of the leafy portion of the stem. Keep about 3 to 4 inches of the stem, and remove all leaves from the stems. Make a flat surface at the root end so that it will be easy to set up.

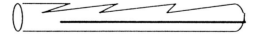

Make diagonal cuts along the length of each stem about two thirds deep, being careful not to cut through to the other side of the stem.

Cut the thick stem lengthwise into 2 or 3 strips leaving one inch uncut at the base (the root end). Soak the garnish in ice water for several hours so that the stem strips will "blossom." Cut a section of carrot, about one inch, to form the center. Cut the carrot into 1/16-inch strips, but do not cut all the way through. Rotate 90 degrees and repeat, creating a checkerboard effect.

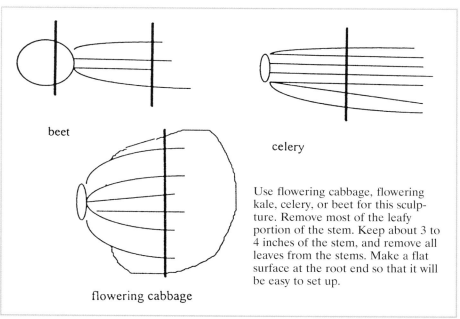

beet

celery

flowering cabbage

Use flowering cabbage, flowering kale, celery, or beet for this sculpture. Remove most of the leafy portion of the stem. Keep about 3 to 4 inches of the stem, and remove all leaves from the stems. Make a flat surface at the root end so that it will be easy to set up.

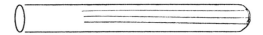

Cut the thick stem lengthwise into very thin strips leaving a one-inch uncut base. Soak the garnish in ice water for several hours so that the stem strips will "blossom."

Flowering-maple

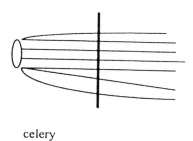

celery

Use a 3- to 4-inch base of a celery stalk for this garnish.

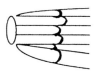

celery

Carve each stem to a petal shape. Start outside and work in for about 9 to 10 stems. Remove the center and replace with a radish garnish or any kind of berry.

Take a stalk of rhubarb.

Peel one end and carve to a head shape. Insert 2 whole cloves into the face as eyes. Cut the other end lengthwise into very thin strips leaving one inch uncut. Soak the garnish in ice water for several hours so that the tentacles will become curly arms.

Mushrooms

Azalea

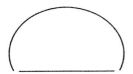

Remove the stem of a button mushroom.

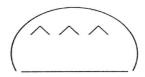

Press lightly on the center of the mushroom with the tip of a knife to create triangular impressions in a circular pattern as the first row of petals (as illustrated).

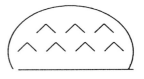

Continue with a second and third row of petals if space permits, alternating the petals with each row.

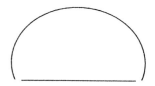

Remove the stem of a button mushroom.

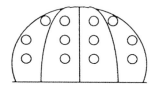

Make three to four circular impressions in each area. Take a small rectangle of yellow bell pepper and cut into thin strips along long side, almost to end. Fold and insert uncut end into top of mushroom to imitate stamen.

Using the dull side or back of a knife, indent the mushroom top into eight areas.

Onion

Lotus Flower

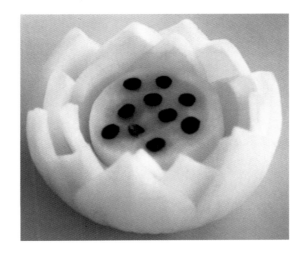

Cut 7 or 8 deep V-shaped petals depending on the size of your onion.

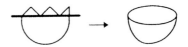

Leaving the petals intact, cut the central layers of the onion to about 2/3 the height of the petals; this will be the lotus seedpod.

Remove the top.

Cut about 10 small circles out of the skin of a cucumber and put them on the top of the lotus seedpod as lotus seeds.

Cut an onion apart by making deep V-shaped cuts into the center of the bulb of the onion with a sharp knife. Make them as long and as thin as possible leaving a half-inch base. Soak in cold water for at least one hour, this will produce a bloom.

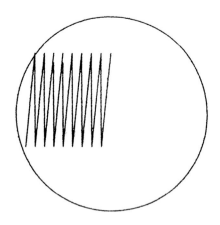

Zucchinis and Squash

Flower Basket

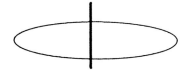

Cut a zucchini in half.

Stab the basket body's skin to several upside down V-shapes. Fold the resulting V-shaped skins back.

Carve a basket shape out of the half zucchini. Cut the edge of the basket with a V-carving tool. Carve the handle of the basket with a knife (as illustrated).

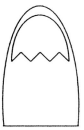

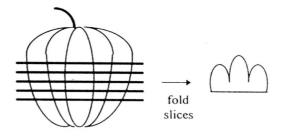

fold
slices

Slice an acorn squash horizontally into thin slices.
Remove the seeds from each slice and fold in half.
Roll one slide into a cylinder, then continue to wrap
the folded slices around cylinder one by one,
arranging the petals around the core. You will be
working with the skin side of the slice facing down
and seed side of the slice facing up.

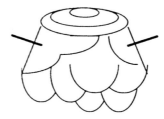

Secure the base with toothpicks.
Turn the garnish over to its
upright position. Fold the edges
of the petals back.

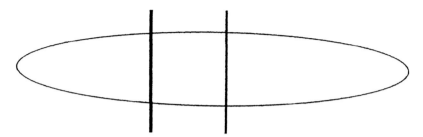

Take a two-inch section from the middle of a yellow squash or zucchini.

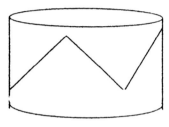

Carve 3 petals around it as a first row of petals, about 1/16-inch deep.

Shape the rest of the material to a horn or spool shape.

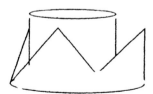

Sharpen the remaining material into a cylinder. Following the same procedure as before, make a second row of petals. The rows of petals should be alternated.

Carve a little cylinder out of carrot and insert it into the middle of the horn. You can be creative with the central garnish.

Tropical bird

Cut a zucchini in half. Slice it into thirds lengthwise.

Carve a parrot out of the smaller slice. Attach to a lemon stand using toothpicks, and use smaller zucchini as tail feathers.

Eggplants

Little Boat

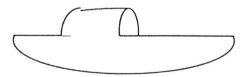

Carve an eggplant into a boat shape. Carve a seat and hollow inside.

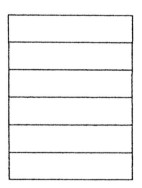

Cut a rectangle for a sail out of carrot and carve grooves on it with a V-carving tool. Pierce the sail with a skewer and insert into the boat.

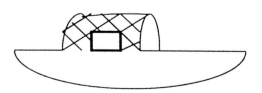

Carve diamond-grooves on the cabin with a V-carving tool. Cut a square on the each side of the cabin for windows.

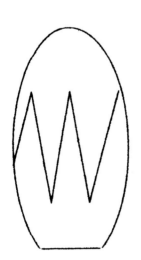

Slice the petals to two layers.

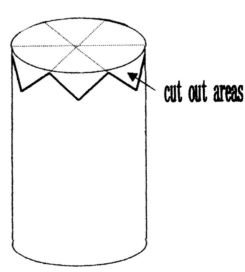

cut out areas

Carve six petals, a quarter-inch deep, around an eggplant and remove the top half.

Carve the rest of the meat to a cylinder. Make six V-shaped cuts on the cylinder top with a V-carving tool. Soak the garnish in lemon water to prevent the inner meat from turning brown.

Goldfish

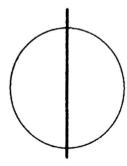

Cut a tomato in half
vertically.

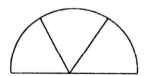

Cut the half tomato into three
wedges.

Separate two thirds of the
skin from the two side wedges
as the gold fish's fins; Leave
the middle wedge as the gold
fish's body.

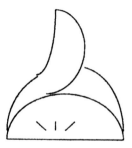

  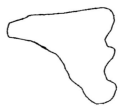

Cut three slices out of onion for the tail.

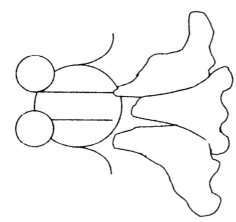

Use two cherry tomatoes for eyes, and put them in the front of the body. Put the three tails behind the body, as illustrated.

Poppy

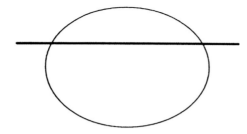

Cut a tomato in half horizontally. Remove the top part of the tomato and hollow it out, leaving about a quarter inch around the edge.

Separate the skin from the meat almost to the base of the tomato. Make two rows of petals. Carve the skin into two petals; carve the meat layer into two petals. Alternate the two rows of petals. Insert filaments cut from cucumber skin into the center of the garnish.

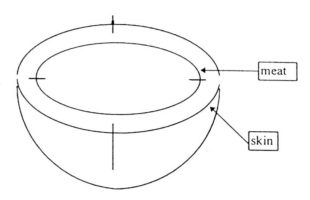

meat

skin

Water Lily

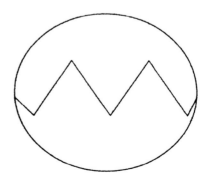

Take a red tomato and a smaller green tomato. Carve 5 petals around each tomato.

Remove the inner meat of the red tomato and place the green tomato in its center.

Dogwood Flower

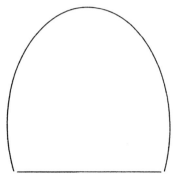

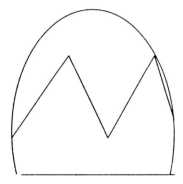

Use Roma tomatoes for this garnish. Remove the bottom to make the garnish stable.

Carve four petals around the tomato as illustrated. Separate to two parts so two flowers can be made out of one tomato. Remove the seeds from each half but keep the meat in the center. Create leaves using cucumber skins carved with a V-tool.

Cucumbers

Sunflower

Remove both ends of a cucumber. Insert a
chopstick or a skewer lengthwise through the
center of the cucumber.

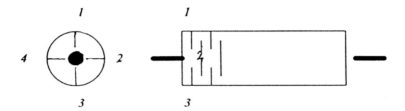

Imagine there are four sides to the cucumber. Opposite sides will be cut at
the same time (sides one and three; sides two and four). Starting at sides
one and three, cut straight down until the knife meets the chopstick or the
skewer about 3/16 of an inch from each end as shown. Then work on sides
two and four, cutting straight down between sides one and three. Continue
cutting the complete length of the cucumber.

Remove the skewer. If you like, you
can remove the seeds to hollow the
cucumber.

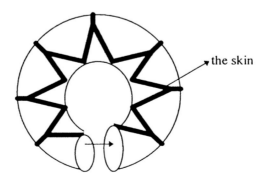

the skin

Gather together both ends of the cucumber and
insert the narrow end into the wide end.

Radishes

Lollipops

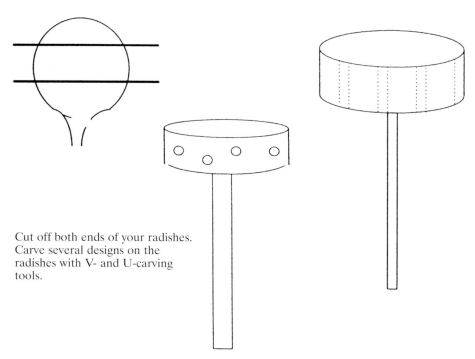

Cut off both ends of your radishes.
Carve several designs on the
radishes with V- and U-carving
tools.

Cut off stem end of the radishes Carve several designs on the radishes with V- and U-carving tools. Insert a toothpick into each carved radish.

Wildflower

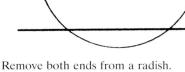

Remove both ends from a radish.

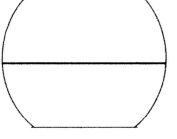

Make a horizontal cut right in the middle around the radish, but not all the way through, leaving about a half-inch diameter in the center uncut.

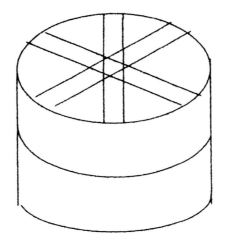

Cut and remove six large wedges from the top to the middle cut leaving the half-inch diameter core intact. Remove the cut off materials.

Wild Chrysanthemum

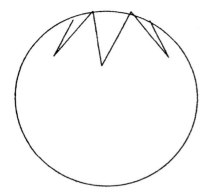

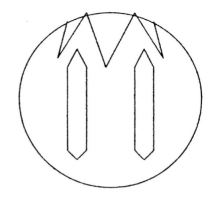

Carve a small flower with a U- or a V-carving tool on a radish top.

Make a straight cut between each small flower petal as illustrated.

Bell Peppers and Hot Peppers

Chinese Fritillaria

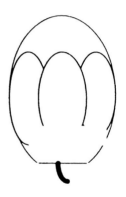

Carve five to six petals around a bell pepper. You have several garnishing options: Take out the seeds and insert some carrot or cucumber filaments, or a whole cherry tomato or a radish in the center. Or leave the seeds in the center as shown, but remove the white connective tissue.

Flower Pot

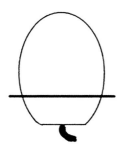

Cut a bell pepper into two parts approximately 1/4 and 3/4 in size, and hollow them. The larger part will be the pot's body and the smaller will be the base.

Put the larger part on top of the smaller part. Make sure the smaller part is stem-end up while the larger part should be end down. Carve the rim of the pot with a V-shaped edge.

Palm Tree

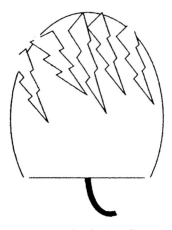

Carve connected palm tree leaves around a green bell pepper with a knife. Remove the stem end and keep the non-stem end as tree leaves.

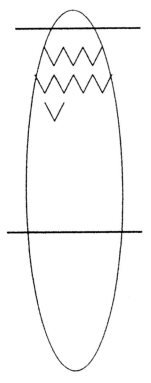

Carve a tree trunk from a carrot section with a U-carving tool. Starting at the smaller end, carve individual U-shaped cuts around the carrot to create rows. Attach the tree leaves on the smaller end of the trunk with toothpicks. Carve a rock out of a potato. Expose it to the air for a while so it will be turn brown, resembling natural rock.

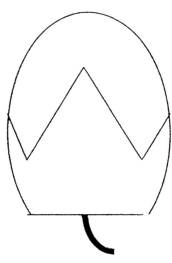

Carve three connected petals around a green bell pepper leaving the stem on as illustrated, and separate to two halves. Put the top half into the bottom half. Both parts should have their skin side down and the petals should alternate.

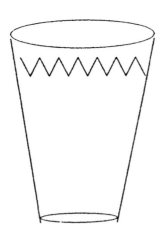

Carve rows of connected V-shapes around a section of carrot from the larger end to the smaller end with a V-shaped tool, alternating the V's with each row until ¼ inch is left at the smaller end. Carve the final ¼ inch portion into a small flower shape. Insert the finished carrot into the middle of the pepper petals with a toothpick.

Nerine

Carve connected V-shapes around a red bell pepper with a knife for petals. Make the petals as thin as you can. Trim out the white connective tissue but leave the seeds attached. Soak the garnish in ice water for several hours so that the petals will curve.

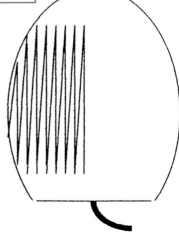

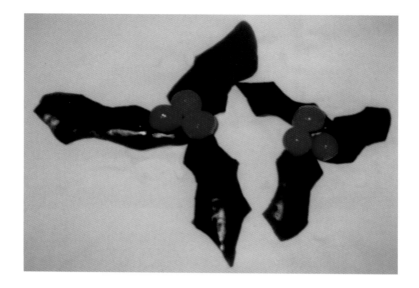

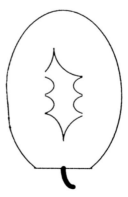

Carve English Holly leaves out of
green bell pepper or zucchini skin.
Put several cherries in the middle
of three leaves.

Root Vegetables

All root vegetables can be used for the following designs, such as carrots, Turnips, Kohlrabi, potatoes, sweet potatoes, beets, and daikon radish.

Showy Peony

Shape the material to a half-ball with a knife.

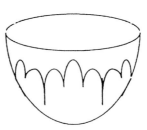

Carve each edge of the flat surface into a petal shape (as illustrated). Starting behind the same flat surface where the paring began, carve petals around the half-ball. These will be the first row of petals.

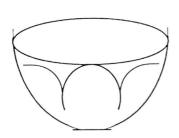

Pare five flat surfaces around the half-ball.

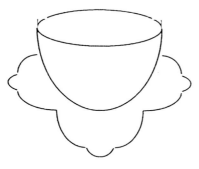

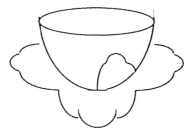

Shape the rest of the material to a half-ball again.

Follow the same procedure as before, the rows of petals should be alternated. Make two or three rows of petals until the center of the half-ball becomes 2/5-inch in diameter. Stab filaments in the center of the core with a V-carving tool. Soak the garnish in cold water until ready for use. The water may be colored with food coloring.

Rhododendron

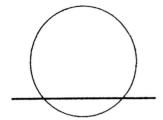

Use a turnip or radish and cut the stem end flat in order to stabilize the garnish. (Turnip has a nice color and good shape for this garnish. Other materials need shaping first.)

Carve a circle on the top center and stab a few holes with the hole maker in the center of the circle.

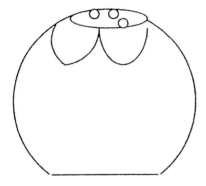

Each petal

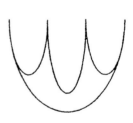

Carve four leaves around the circle. There are two steps to do this. First, make three connected U-shaped cuts with a U-carving tool for each leaf, then, right behind the first cut, make a very thin second cut in the same way. The first row will show up.

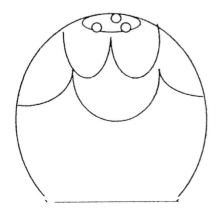

Follow the same procedure as before, the rows of petals should be alternated. The second and third rows need five connected U-shaped cuts for each leaf so that there are still four leaves in each row.

Dianthus

Cut three to eleven
carrot, purple
potato, cucumber,
beet, or turnip slices.

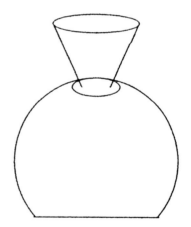

Use an apple, orange, tomato, or potato
as a base. Cut one end flat so that it easily
sets up. Carve one to three holes in the
other end. Each hole will hold one flower.

Put the pointy end of the
cone into the hole and one
by one turn down each
slice to make petals. Use
toothpicks to secure the
petals. Insert an olive,
grape, berry, radish, or
cherry tomato, depending
on the colors desired, into
the center.

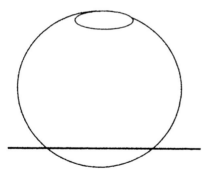

Spread the slices out on a flat surface and roll into a cone.

Peacock

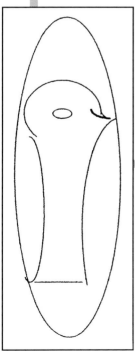

Carve a head and neck out of a section of
Daikon radish. Insert two whole cloves
into the face as eyes and cut out a mouth.
Carve a crest out of a piece of carrot and
insert into the top of the head. Rest the
bird on Chinese cabbage leaves and
garnish with slices of colorful bell peppers.

Calla Lily

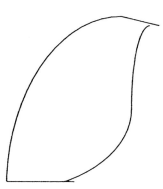

Cut a 2 x 4 x ¼ inch slice carrot and shape as illustrated.

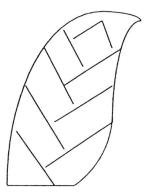

Carve large V-shapes on both sides. Each cut must be at 45 degrees. Insert it in bokchoy with a toothpick.

Alley Cat

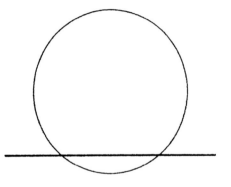

Stabilize a turnip by making a flat cut on the stem end.

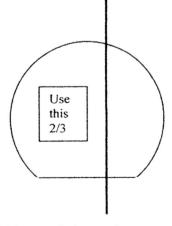

Make a vertical cut and remove 1/3 of the turnip.

Use this 2/3

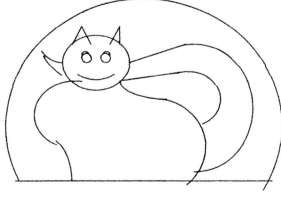

Carve a cat out of the remaining part. Make sure the cat's tail is behind the body.

Chapter 4
Simple Fruit Carving

Used in garnishing and decorating single-order and small-party fruit trays and desert platters.

Papayas

Zinnia

Alcantarea (made out of both papaya and cucumber)

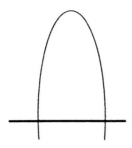

Remove one end
of a papaya.

Carve connected, deep V-
shapes around the papaya.
Separate into two halves
and remove the seeds.

Take one half and
carve an upside down
V-shape underneath
the first V-shapes,
cutting through the
skin only.

Separate the skin and the meat
only between the first and second
v-shaped cutting area. Then cut
the meat into 2 or 3 layers. Insert
some filaments made out of
another vegetable into the middle
of the garnish.

Citrus Fruit

Butterfly

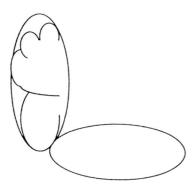

Carve two butterfly wings out of a piece of lemon skin. Stab some circles in them with a hole maker for decoration.

Cut two sticks as antennae and put them on the front of the body.

Marlin

Slice away one-third of an orange.

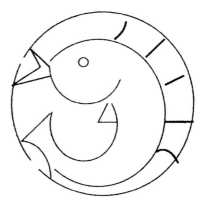

Carve a marlin on the rind of the third.

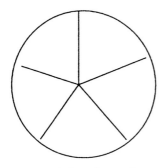

Cut an apple into five wedges.

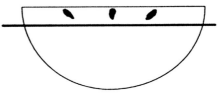

Remove the seeds with a horizontal cut as shown. This will allow the wedge to stand skin-side up.

Carve a big V-shape just through the skin as illustrated and remove the stem-end skin.

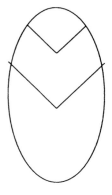

Carve another V-shape above the first V-shape and deeper than the first cut. Remove about 1/8-inch of meat from the stem end. Do this to all five wedges. Soak in lemon water to prevent browning. To display, lay them skin up in a circle.

Barrel Cactus

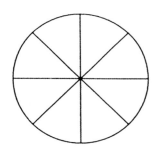

Cut an apple horizontally at the non-stem end and slice into eight wedges.

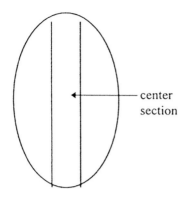

center section

Make two skin-deep straight cuts length-wise along each wedge.

Remove skin from both sides to the cut on each wedge and then reassemble the apple. Put a blueberry on top.

Honeydew

Turtle

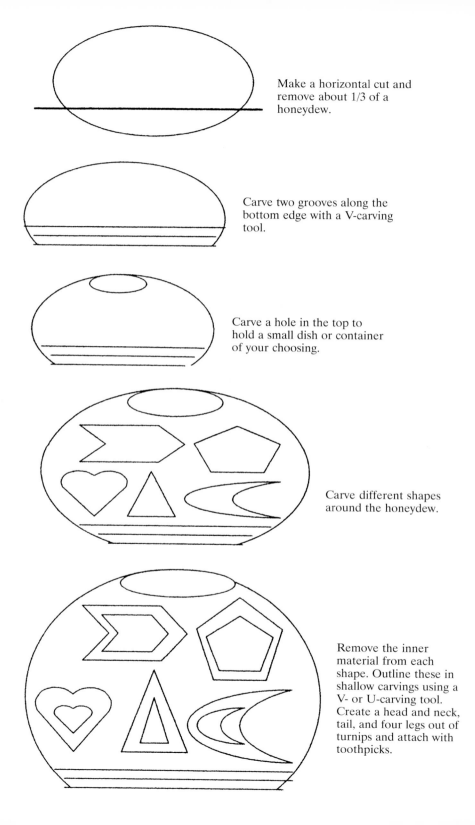

Make a horizontal cut and remove about 1/3 of a honeydew.

Carve two grooves along the bottom edge with a V-carving tool.

Carve a hole in the top to hold a small dish or container of your choosing.

Carve different shapes around the honeydew.

Remove the inner material from each shape. Outline these in shallow carvings using a V- or U-carving tool. Create a head and neck, tail, and four legs out of turnips and attach with toothpicks.

Chapter 5

Cold Meat, Cheese, and Egg Carvings

These items are great for garnishing and decorating meat, hors d'oeuvres, and tea sandwich platters.

Rose

Take one slice and roll it, like a jellyroll to form the core.

Cut roast beef or ham into thin rectangular slices, about 4 x 2.5 inches. You will need 24 slices.

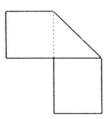

Fold the rest of the slices in half as shown. While holding the core in your hand, space the folded slices around the core as petals. The folded angle will form the top of the petal. Continue placing the petals until 24 folded slices have been put in place. Insert a toothpick through the bottom of the garnish to hold the petals in place.

Rosebud

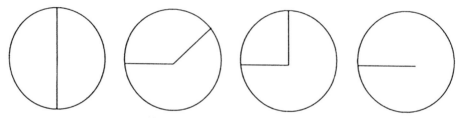

You will need twelve thick slices of salami or bologna. Group these three slices to a unit. Cut the slices of the first unit in half. Remove 1/3 from the slices of the second unit. Remove 1/4 from the slices of the third unit. Make a radial cut in the fourth unit.

Overlap the pointed ends of each slice of the first unit to form a conical shape.

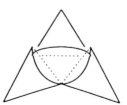

Put the three conical shapes together to form a triangular shape attaching them with a toothpick. This will be the first row of petals. Continue by adding the second, third and fourth units on the same toothpick to create three more rows of petals.

Marigold

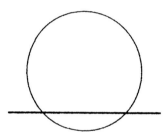

Slice a section of salami or beet horizontally into thin slices. Cut one-third off as illustrated.

Wrap the rest of the slices around the cylinder one by one (arrange the petals around the core). You will be working with the round side of the slice facing down and the flat side of the slice facing up.

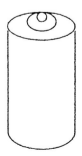

Roll the first slice into a cylinder.

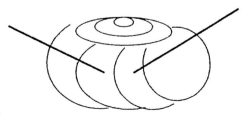

Secure the base of flat sides with toothpicks. Put some small herb leaves into the center. Turn the garnish over to its upright position. Fold the edges of the petals back.

Children

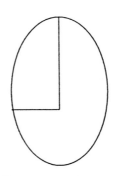
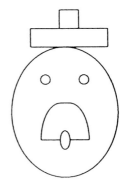

Remove a section from the upper part of a boiled egg as illustrated. The yolk will be the little child's face.

Carve a hat, tongue, and eyes out of a carrot. You may also use two black peppercorns for the eyes.

Playing Fish

Cut a hard-boiled egg in half lengthwise. Carve side fins from a slice of carrot, as shown. Also, create a mouth and eyes from small pieces of carrot.

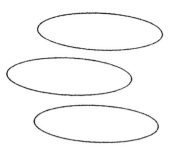

Carve three tailfins out of bell pepper and put them behind the body.

Rabbit

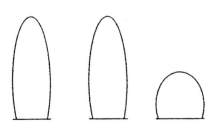

Carve two long ears and a tongue out of a piece of red bell pepper and attach to hard-boiled egg.

Insert two whole cloves into the face as eyes.

108

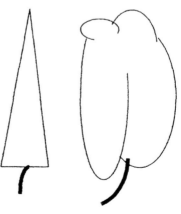

Carve the shapes of different kinds of hot peppers such as jalapeño, cherry, New Mexico, Chinese Chaotian hot pepper, and Habanero from different cheeses, including hot pepper cheese, Gouda cheese, and cheddar cheese. Insert a real pepper stem.

Clematis

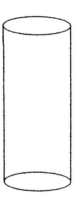

Cut a piece of
semi-soft cheese
into a small
cylinder.

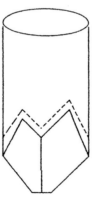

Make a deep cut
behind each
inclined plane to
form petals. Cut
through the point
of the square awl to
form a small
flower. Put a berry
into the center of
the small flower.
Continue to create
flowers up the
cylinder.

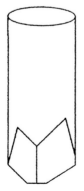

Pare four inclined
planes on the end
of the cylinder so
that it makes a
square awl on the
end.

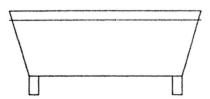

Carve a bonsai pot out of a block of semi-soft cheese. Carve an irregular stone about twice the height of the pot out of a different color of semi-soft cheese using V- and U-carving tools and a hole maker. Create grasses and little flowers out of cheese. Assemble the pot, the stone, flowers, and grasses using toothpicks.

Evening Primrose

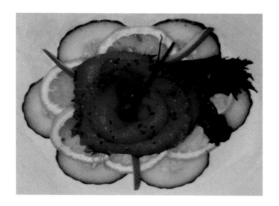

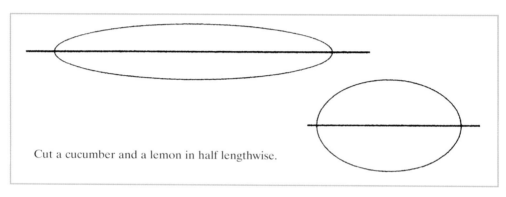

Cut a cucumber and a lemon in half lengthwise.

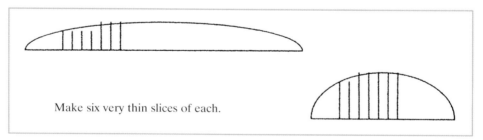

Make six very thin slices of each.

Arrange them to make a base. Take four or five slices of smoked salmon and some vegetable strips as stamen. Roll the salmon slices around the stamen in the same way as the marigold.

Chapter 6

Dough Sculpture

This form of art is great for decorating desert plates, trays, and the table itself.

Chinese Decoration Dough

½ c. sweet rice, ground
2 c. all purpose flour
½ c. cake flour
warm water
1 Tbs. oil
1 Tbs. honey
food colors

1. Combine the water with ground sweet rice, all purpose flour, and cake flour. Create a smooth thin paste.
2. Leave the dough covered for an hour.
3. Steam the covered dough for 30 to 40 minutes.
4. After the dough cools down a little bit, knead in the oil, honey, and food colors until smooth.

This dough is very good for sculpting. After 5 to 7 days of air-drying it will keep forever. Although edible, it does not taste good. This dough is wonderful for many kinds of handicrafts that require great detail, but making the dough is time consuming.

To finish your project and make it shine, coat with a light layer of cooking oil.

Panda

A Little Mouse Carries a Huge Peanut

Santa

Salt Dough

1 c. water, cold
1 c. cornstarch.
1 c. salt
butter, honey, as needed

1. Combine the water with cornstarch.
2. Bring the mixture to a boil and cook to create a smooth thick paste.
3. Knead in the salt, butter, and honey until smooth.
   This dough is easy to make and good for making crafts because after 5 to 7 days of air-drying it will keep forever. After drying some salt will come to the surface so it doesn't look as good as the Chinese decoration dough. It is good for white decorations of different sizes.

Swan

Iced Sugar Cookie Dough

3-¼ c. all-purpose flour
½ tsp. baking powder
½ tsp. salt
2 ½ sticks unsalted butter, softened
1 c. sugar
1 each large egg
1 tsp. milk
2 ½ tsp. Vanilla
Food coloring as needed

1. Whisk flour, baking powder, and salt together thoroughly. Set aside.
2. In large bowl, beat butter and sugar on medium speed until very fluffy and well blended:
3. Add egg, milk, and vanilla to the butter/sugar mixture and beat until well combined.
4. Gradually stir the flour mixture into the butter mixture until well blended and smooth. Finally, add the food coloring. Refrigerate until cold and slightly firm.
5. Make garnishes.
6. Preheat the oven to 375°F. Bake garnishes 10 to 15 minutes, or until they are evenly and lightly browned.

This dough is for making bigger garnishes to decorate the dessert table. It is also very good for children's parties and nursing home activities because it tastes good. As a party activity, children can play with the dough, bake it, and then eat their work. This dough can be used to make many kinds of flowers, animals, and cartoon characters. Have fun!

Sugar Cookie Roses

Steps:
1. Make fourteen petals out of the dough.
2. Take the first petal and fold in half lengthwise for the center.
3. Wrap three petals around the center as the first row of petals.
4. Continue adding the second and third rows but with five petals to each row. Alternate the petals.
5. Finally fold the petals back to make them look natural.

Chapter 7
Pasta Garnishes

Decorating the Buffet

These garnishes are the only ones you can not eat in this book. They are uncooked and use non-toxic glue. They are useful for decorating a pasta table.

Angels

Body made of a piece of rigatoni. Wings made of a piece of farfalle. Head made of a piece conchigliette, with both ends removed. I use sharp wire cutters for this job. Sometimes the pasta will crack or break, so make sure you have extra pieces. Arms made of elbow macaroni.

Seashore

Sail and boat body made of pieces of lasagne. Mast made of a piece of canneloni. Seashells made of some pieces of conchigliette, conchiglie, and cavatappi. Sand made of breadcrumbs.

Wagon

Wheels made of rotini. Handles made of two pieces of spaghetti. Wagon body made of a piece of lasagne.

Friends

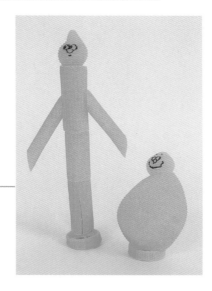

Head made of a piece of conchigliette (remove one end for the short one). The short, stout figure made of a piece of conchiglie (remove one end), and the tall, slender figure made of three pieces of rigatoni. Arms made of penne. The base is made from a piece of rotini.

A Buffoon

Hat made of a piece of rotini and a piece of conchigliette (remove one end). Head made of a piece of conchiglie (remove one end). Hair made of some pieces of vermicelli. Mouth made of a piece of elbow macaroni.

Chapter 8
Sculpting Small Melons and Squash

Used for garnishing and decorating hors d'oeuvre and crudités trays or other small size party trays. Most round shaped garnishes can be used as containers for toothpicks placed on the serving tray for guests to pick up food on the tray, or as containers for dipping sauces. The basic techniques used are hollow sculpture and relief sculpture. The former is carved through the whole wall including the skin and the meat, the latter only carved through the skin, with part of the skin removed.

Soapwort Flower

Engrave a soapwort flower image on the skin of a honeydew. Carve an outside row of petals using the hollow sculpture technique, and other rows of petals with the relief sculpture technique.

Daisy

Use a small pumpkin or cantalope for this garnishing. Remove the skin of the center area where the flower form will be. Carve the flower shape into the skinless area. Carve the petals holding a knife at a 40 to 50 degree angle.

Chrysanthemum

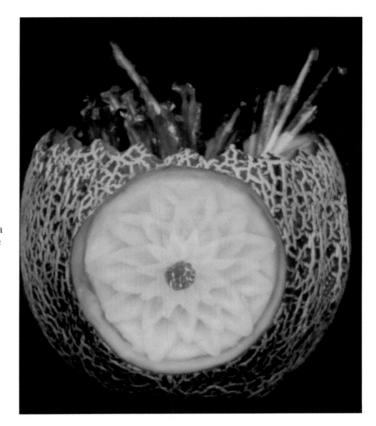

Remove the skin of a cantaloupe in a large circle where the chrysanthemum will be, but leave a small circle in the center. Carve a chrysanthemum on the skinless area with different size V-carving tools.

Happy Family

Engrave three parrot images on the skin of a small pumpkin using the relief sculpture technique.

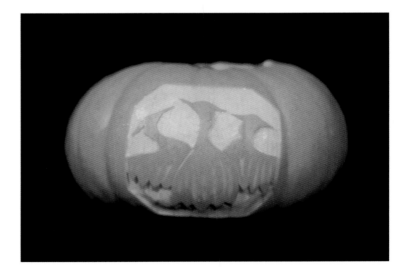

————————

Engrave a design on the
skin of a small pumpkin
with the relief sculpture
technique.

———————— Happiness

Carve the Chinese character
"happiness" on an acorn squash
skin using the relief sculpture
technique.

Longevity ————————

Engrave a red-crowned crane image with a
Chinese character "longevity" on the skin
of a small pumpkin using the relief
sculpture technique. Cranes can live for 60
years, so they symbolize longevity.

This is a very popular symbol in China. The yin-yang represents opposites, while the ba-gua represents heaven, earth, thunder, wind, water, fire, mountains, and lakes. Choose a green-skinned cantaloupe for this garnish. Engrave the image on the cantaloupe skin using the relief sculpture technique. In order to make a distinction between yin-yang and ba-gua, the center yin-yang part is carved with the whole skin and no skin; the ba-gua symbol is carved with the green skin (which is revealed by removing a thin layer of rough skin) and no skin.

African Violet

Remove the skin of an acorn squash where the African violet will be and carve an African violet in it.

Orchid

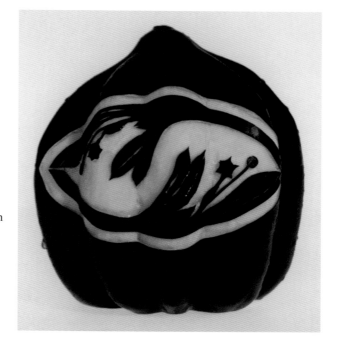

Engrave two opposite orchid images on the skin of an acorn squash with the relief sculpture technique.

Grapes

Choose a green-skinned cantaloupe for this garnish. There are three layers to be carved. The first layer is the carving of the leaves and vines. Some of them retain their skin, while some of them retain the inner green and smooth skin. The second layer comprises the grapes. The skin should be totally removed. The third layer is background, just remove more meat and smooth it out. This garnish can either remain a whole cantaloupe or make a hole on the top and remove the seeds to create a container for fruit salad or fruit dip.

White Trillium

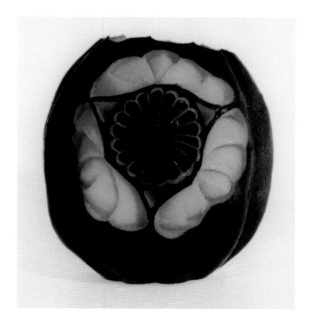

Engrave the image of a white trillium on the skin of an acorn squash with the relief sculpture technique. Remove the skin around the center and carve three petals.

Insert various garnishes on an eggplant base.

Chapter 9
Sculpting Large Melons and Squash

Used for garnishing and decorating fruit, cheese and other trays at large parties. Some of them may be used as fruit salad containers. The basic techniques are the same as before.

Happy New Year

Engrave the image of a clock on a pumpkin skin with the relief sculpture technique. The flowers located in the four corners should be carved deeper. Carve the words "new year" on the top and bottom of the clock.

Wedding

Choose a butternut squash with a short neck and a large body for this garnish. Peel the neck and half the body. Carve a wedding couple out of the neck and the lady's wedding gown out of the upper half of the squash body.

Loving Kiss

Engrave the image of a pair of mandarin ducks kissing underneath a Chinese lotus on a watermelon skin. Carve the mandarins using the hollow sculpture technique and the relief sculpture technique for carving the lotus.

Carve five petals around a cantaloupe, cutting clear through the meat and separate into two parts. Carve leaves out of the top portion and then turn upside down to act as a base. Hollow each petal of the bowl to make it pretty and allow light to pass through. Different candles will create a different glow.

Happy Birthday

This garnish is for a children's birthday party. Engrave the images of five deer on a half pumpkin skin using the relief sculpture technique. Make five holes on top to hold candles. Hollow some designs between the deer so that if you put a candle inside the pumpkin the light will shine through.

An Embrace

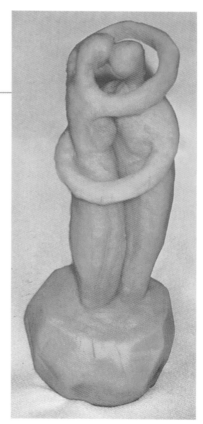

Choose a long-neck butternut squash for this garnish. Peel it and remove the seeds. Make a base out of the butternut squash body. Carve a couple hugging each other out of the neck.

Poinsettia Jar

Watermelons have red and green colors and so are perfect materials for carving Christmas garnishes. Carve a Christmas lantern out of a watermelon using both the relief and hollow sculpture techniques. Leave the watermelon skin on as the poinsettia leaves and stems. Carve stamens out of a piece of carrot, and assemble them on the poinsettia.

Cardinal on Holly

Engrave the image of a
cardinal perched on a
holly branch on the rind
of a watermelon using
the hollow sculpture
technique.

Reindeer Lantern

Engrave the image of a
reindeer on the skin of
a pumpkin using the
relief sculpture
technique. Hollow
carve around the
reindeer to make a
lantern.

Engrave the image of a
church on the skin of a
watermelon using the
relief sculpture technique.
Hollow carve around the
church to make a lantern.

Church Bells

Engrave an image of a church with a bell tower on a watermelon using the relief sculpture technique. Carve the doors using the hollow sculpture technique so that they look like they are halfway open.

July Fourth

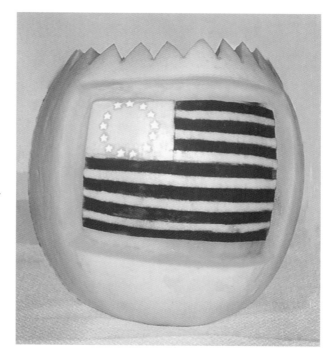

Engrave the image of an American Flag on the skin of a honeydew using the relief sculpture technique. Dye the stripes with red food coloring.

Bald Eagle

Engrave the image of a Bald
Eagle on the skin of a
butternut squash using the
relief sculpture technique.

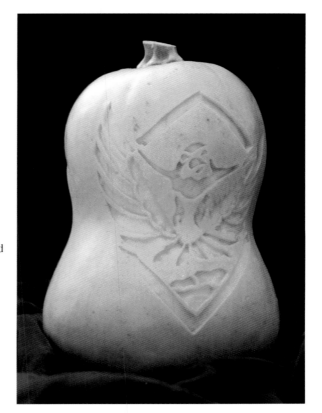

Happy Thanksgiving

Engrave the image of two
maple leaves and the
words "Happy Thanksgiv-
ing" on the skin of a
pumpkin using the relief
sculpture technique.

Engrave the image of a little girl with a few pumpkins around her on the skin of a watermelon using the relief sculpture technique. Hollow the outline of the girl to make the sculpture more colorful.

Turkey

Remove non-stem end of a pumpkin and save it for carving a wing. Engrave the images of a turkey, a pumpkin, and leaves on the skin of the pumpkin using the relief sculpture technique. Hollow the outline of the turkey so that light can pass through. Sculpt a wing out of the bottom piece using a U-carving tool, and attach to the turkey with a toothpick.

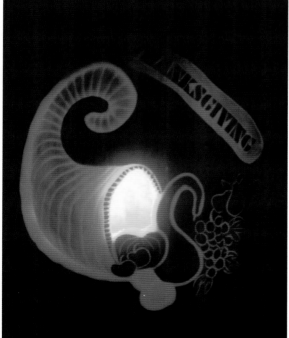

Engrave the image of a cornucopia, a pumpkin, and fruits in the skin of a pumpkin using the relief sculpture technique. Then remove the skin of the cornucopia and hollow the cornucopia mouth to make it look three-dimensional.

Use ice-carving tools for this project. Engrave the image of a face on the skin of a gigantic pumpkin with the hollow sculpture technique. Make some simple decorative holes around the pumpkin so that light can pass through evenly. Put some corn leaves on top of the pumpkin for hair.

Hollow carve a moon and engrave stars, ghosts, and bats on the skin of a pumpkin using the relief sculpture technique to make a lantern.

Hearts Linked Together

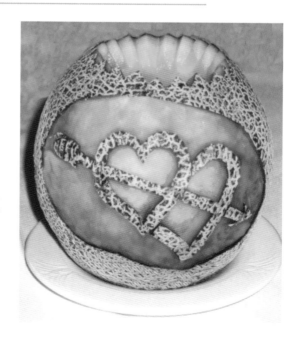

Engrave two images of hearts and an arrow on a cantaloupe skin with the relief sculpture technique.

Dolphins

Carve a dolphin jar out of a watermelon using both the relief and hollow sculpture techniques. Some dolphins are carved on white skin, and some on the dark skin. Seaweed is carved on white skin.

Carve a chrysanthemum bowl out of a watermelon. The leaves are carved using the relief sculpture technique. The flowers are carved on the fruit using different size V-carving tolls. This can be used as a fruit salad container or, if you continue to hollow the vase, it makes a beautiful votive candle holder.

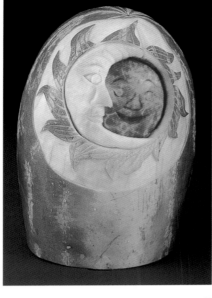

Sun and Moon

Engrave images of the moon on
a watermelon skin and the sun
on the fruit.

Waterfall by Mountain Pavilion

Engrave images of mountains,
rock, a pavilion, a pine, and a
natural stone bridge on the skin of
a watermelon. Soak one half
pound of dried Chinese green bean
starch noodles in warm water. Put
the softened noodles underneath
the natural stone bridge as a
waterfall. Remove the stems of
broccoli and soak them in very hot
water for a half-minute. Cool them
down, and insert them into the
mountain as vegetation with
toothpicks. Hang some fresh herbs
as ivy.

Goldfish Lantern

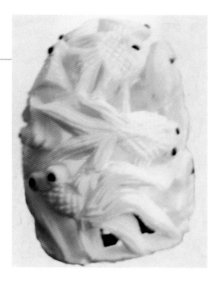

Peel a large zucchini. Engrave images of gold fish around the zucchini using the hollow sculpture technique. Insert black peppercorns into the fish faces as eyes.

The Sailing Boat

Engrave the image of a sailboat on the skin of a watermelon using the relief sculpture technique.

Tropical Sea Scene

Carve coconut palms, sailboats, and submerged rocks on a watermelon skin. Remove the dark skin between the palms and rocks but leave the light skin on for carving the ocean water. Finally, remove all the skin above the water to expose the red meat as sky.

Melon Lantern

Use the special melon lantern sculpture technique for these lantern designs.

145

Chinese Character "Blessing"

Carve the Chinese Character "Blessing" on the side of a watermelon with the hollow sculpture technique. Remove most of the meat, but not all, so that three colors will show.

Beautiful Lady

Choose a light green pumpkin for this garnish. Engrave the image of a pretty lady on the skin of the pumpkin using the relief sculpture technique.

Pretty Girl

Engrave the image of a pretty girl on the skin of a butternut squash using the relief sculpture technique.

Basket of Flowers

Carve a basket shape out of a watermelon. Carve some U-shapes along the handle's edges and basket body's edge. Carve some large upside down V-shapes and hollow some holes between the V-shapes around the basket body for decoration. Fill your basket with real or sculpted flowers for a beautiful centerpiece.

Above: Carve a basket shape out of a small watermelon. Put two thicker slices of pineapple on the basket edge horizontally to increase the area of the basket. Insert flowers on the pineapple slices and the basket handle.

Welcome ———————————

Cut a watermelon in half for this garnish. The dark green skin makes luscious flower leaves while the flower petals come alive with the light green skin and red meat. Carve two flowers, one on top and the other on the side. Between the flowers carve the word "welcome."

Use a piece of "useless" watermelon rind for this garnish. Engrave images of a palm tree, ocean, a sail, rock, and a pavilion using the relief sculpture technique.

Squirrels ————

Choose a curved neck pumpkin for this garnish. Carve two squirrels on the neck of the pumpkin. Carve some pine leaves on the green skin (peel off the very thin outside skin to get to the green skin). Carve a hole into the trunk and put some nuts underneath the pine.

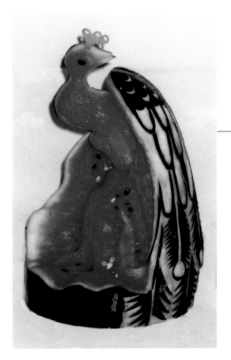

———— *Peacock*

Carve the peacock head, neck, and body in the watermelon meat so that the bird is red. Carve his tail feathers on the watermelon skin.

Use about an eight-inch diameter Daikon radish for this garnish. Sculpt the dragon head, body, and tail separately. Connect the three parts with toothpicks. Carve the dragon tongue out of a carrot and a ball out of Daikon. Insert the ball and the tongue into the dragon mouth. Carve the palace out of another piece of Daikon radish, and put on the boat.

Logos

Carve a logo of your choice on a cantaloupe using the relief sculpture technique.

Swan

Choose an oblong honeydew for this garnish. Carve the swan neck and head on the top of the honeydew without the skin. Carve two wings on the sides with skin so that the feathers can be carved in the skin. Carve the tail on the other end of the honeydew without the meat so they can be spread out.

Chapter 10
Sculpting Hard Cheese and Tallow

These large sculptures can be put on the center table of a buffet or party for visual excitement.

Spicy Tallow Christmas Tree

Steps:

1. Glue one Styrofoam stick and six Styrofoam cups together to make a tree-like object. The stick will be the tree trunk and the cups will form the branches.

2. Mix dill with tallow for foliage material and cover the center supporter cups with it. Completely cover the cups and carve a real tree shape out of the dill tallow. Carve additional branches and put them around the tree.

3. Mix ground cinnamon and cocoa powder with tallow to make tree trunk material and cover the center stick with it. Carve it to look like a real tree trunk. Include some roots.

4. Mix paprika with tallow to make the red color for Santa's coat.

Use spices, nuts and dried fruits to decorate the tree. Some good examples are pink peppercorns, whole cloves, whole coriander, dried Mexican hot pepper, Chinese star anise, peanuts, hazelnuts, dried cranberries, dried apricot, and dried sour cherries. The finished tree stands 2-1/2 feet tall.

Above: Humpty-Dumpty Sitting on the Wall at the 1998 International Hotel Olympics held in London, England. The sculpture is two feet high. The author sculpted the Humpty-Dumpty, but not the wall. The body was sculpted from a whole block of tallow using the three dimensional method.

The arm, two legs, hat, and the feather were carved separately.

Spicy Tallow Sleigh

Steps:

1. Glue two styrofoam sticks and boards together to make a support in the shape of a sleigh.

2. Cover the sleigh with tallow.

3. Mix paprika and saffron with tallow for decoration material. Roll the material into strips and put the strips around the sleigh body.

4. Mix ground black pepper and poppy seeds with tallow to make the runners. The finished tray is 3-1/2 feet long by 2 feet wide.

Hard Cheese Logo

Cut a whole Parmigiano (Parmesan) cheese wheel, approximately 2 feet in diameter, into three equal sized discs. Carve a symbol or emblem of your choice on a disc using the relief sculpture technique.

Chapter 11
Sample of Trays with Garnish

Fruit Trays

Watermelon basket with fruit salad.

Chrysanthemum watermelon bowl with fruit salad.

2000 U.S. Senior Open with sliced fruit tray.

Fruit and Cheese Trays

A swan with fruit and cheese tray.

Vegetable Trays

Daikon radish peacock on sliced onion tray.

Cantaloupe carved for 2000 U.S. Senior Open on roasted vegetable tray.

Seafood Trays

Onion flower on salmon tray.

A swan on pâté tray.

Centerpiece with pâté tray.

Chapter 12
Stencils

These stencils are for beginners. You can make a copy of a stencil, which fits your melon or pumpkin size. Tape the stencil on the surface of the melon or pumpkin. Use a sharp knife to carve through the paper and the melon or pumpkin skin along the line. Remove the skin from the white areas and leave skin from the black areas on.

Mountain Pine

Peaks Rising One
Above the Other

The Secluded Valley

Sweet Kiss

Melon carving for
wedding with double
happiness symbol.

Top

165

Good luck parrot, perfect for weddings.

Butterflies

The Great Wall

Carnations

Roses

Chrysanthemums

Hibiscus Flowers

Blessing to All

Auspicious

This black cat symbol turns
bad luck into good.

Grandfather

Symbol for domestic harmony

Character for longevity

Panda

Faun

Postscript

I have been doing art, psychotherapy, and teaching in turn, each of these enriching my life throughout the years. In my art, painting with knives, I create a colorful language in every single work. My first work, psychotherapy, is my art where I receive pleasure when my patients are cured. My other love, teaching, allows me to dispense knowledge with emotion. It is like tending the summer wheat: the more sweat the better the crop. These three loves, just like three primary colors, paint my enriched life.

I published four books and many articles in the psychotherapy

field while in China, but never had the opportunity to do so in food sculpture. Mr. Peter B. Schiffer and Mrs. Tina Skinner of Schiffer Publishing, who have developed a sharp eye for discovering able people, sent a publishing contract to me last spring. My dream, a beautiful hidden-deep-in-my-heart dream, has come true.

Today I am writing this postscript easily and happily. I envision a future filled with more students I can share this art with. I wish to spread my food sculpture knowledge and skill to more and more people, and add more color to the food-decorating field. Anyone devoted to decorating food may reach me at yucitan@yahoo.com.

Index